NATURE ADVENTURES

GOING CANOEING

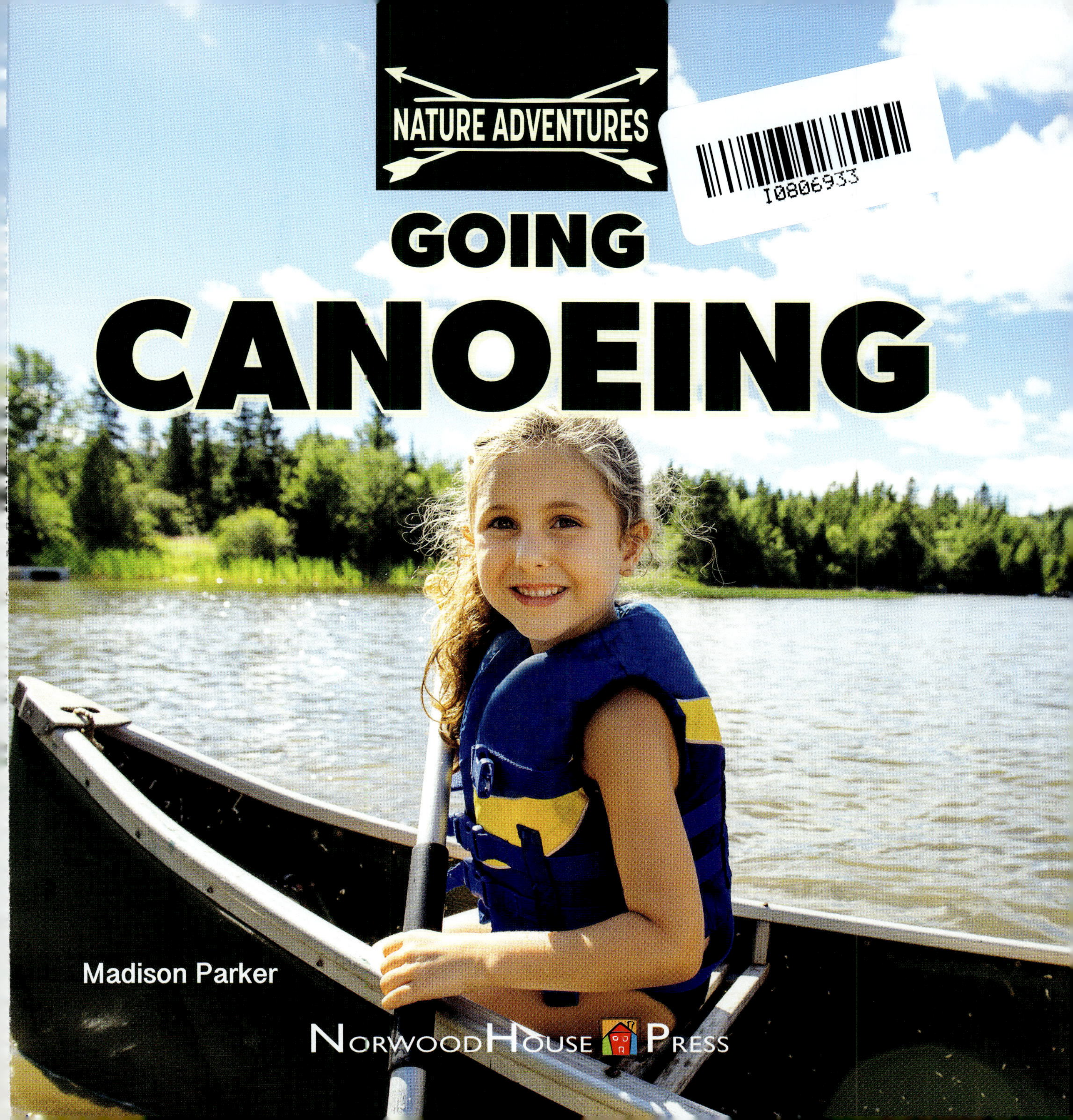

Madison Parker

NorwoodHouse Press

Cataloging-in-Publication Data

Names: Parker, Madison.
Title: Going canoeing / Madison Parker.
Description: Buffalo, NY : Norwood House Press, 2026. | Series: Nature adventures | Includes glossary and index.
Identifiers: ISBN 9781978574625 (pbk.) | ISBN 9781978574632 (library bound) | ISBN 9781978574649 (ebook)
Subjects: LCSH: Canoes and canoeing--Juvenile literature.
Classification: LCC GV784.3 P375 2026 | DDC 797.122--dc23

Published in 2026 by
Norwood House Press
2544 Clinton Street
Buffalo, NY 14224

Designer: Rhea Magaro
Editor: Kim Thompson

Photo credits: Cover, p. 1 Lopolo/Shutterstock.com; p. 5 Erickson Stock/Shutterstock.com; p. 6 Hero Images Inc/Shutterstock.com; p. 7 rjones_photo/Shutterstock.com; p. 8 Randy R/Shutterstock.com; p. 9 New Africa/Shutterstock.com; p. 10 Kellis, Creatus, Hayran1/Shutterstock.com; pp. 11, 16, 19, Dan Thornberg/Shutterstock.com; p. 12 Peter Gudella/Shutterstock.com; p. 13 Max Topchii/Shutterstock.com; pp. 14, 15 r.classen/Shutterstock.com; p. 18 James Kirkikis/Shutterstock.com; p. 21 sofinitaa/Shutterstock.com

Printed in the United States of America

CPSIA compliance information: Batch #CSNHP26: For further information contact Norwood House Press at 1-800-237-9932.

TABLE OF CONTENTS

WHAT IS CANOEING?

Let’s go canoeing! Canoeing is a fun outdoor activity.

A canoe is a long, narrow boat. Most canoes are human-powered.

Canoeing is when people **paddle** a canoe on the water. There are many things to see along the way!

CANOEING SUPPLIES

You will need a canoe. At many parks, you can **rent** a canoe for a few hours. You will also need paddles for moving your canoe through the water.

Every person on the canoe should wear a **life preserver** for safety.

Wear light, comfortable clothes. Water shoes will keep you from slipping. A hat will protect you from the sun.

Pack sunscreen and bug spray. You may want to bring fishing gear. You may want binoculars for spotting animals.

CANOEING SAFETY

Stay safe when you are in a canoe. Do not stand up suddenly. Do not lean over the side. This will keep the canoe from tipping.

Paddles are heavy. Hold on to them tightly. They should not hit anything except the water.

The front of the canoe is the bow. The stern is the back. The right side is the starboard side. The left side is the port side.

The paddler sitting in the bow sets the **pace**. The paddler in the stern **steers**. One paddles starboard, and the other paddles port side. It is important for everyone to stay in their place.

Canoers should Leave No **Trace** (LNT). That means you should not leave trash or anything else behind. Leave the **wilderness** better than you found it. This protects **wildlife**.

WHERE TO GO CANOEING

There are many places to go canoeing. You can canoe on a river, a lake, or a **canal**.

Make sure to read any **regulations** before you go.

Visit your state's park website to find canoeing spots near you. A canoeing trip helps you explore the great outdoors!

Glossary

canal (kuh-NAL): a passage that is dug across land to connect two bodies of water

life preserver (life pri-ZUR-ver): a vest that makes you float in water so that you do not drown

pace (pase): speed

paddle (PAD-uhl): to guide a boat through water by moving a long stick with a flat end

regulations (reg-yuh-LAY-shuhnz): rules you need to follow

rent (rent): to pay for the right to use something for a time

steers (steerz): makes a vehicle travel in a certain direction

trace (trays): a sign that someone has been in a place; evidence

wilderness (WIL-dur-nis): wild land where no people live

wildlife (WILDE-life): wild animals living in their natural environment

Thinking Questions

1. What is canoeing?
2. What makes a canoe move?
3. What are the front and back of a canoe called?
4. How can you stay safe when you go canoeing?
5. Where are some places you can go canoeing?

Index

About the Author

Madison Parker spent her childhood in the city of Chicago, Illinois. A farm girl at heart, today she lives in Wisconsin with her husband and four children on a small farm with cows, goats, chickens, and two miniature horses named Harley and David. Her favorite dessert is vanilla frozen custard with rainbow sprinkles, even in the winter.